Up in the Attic

PAM AYRES

Up in the Attic

EBURY
PRESS

1 3 5 7 9 10 8 6 4 2

Ebury Press, an imprint of Ebury Publishing
20 Vauxhall Bridge Road
London SW1V 2SA

Ebury Press is part of the Penguin Random House group of companies
whose addresses can be found at global.penguinrandomhouse.com

Penguin
Random House
UK

First published by Ebury Press in 2019

www.penguin.co.uk

A CIP catalogue record for this book is available from
the British Library

ISBN 9781529104936

Typeset in 11.25/17 pt Sabon LT Std
by Integra Software Services Pvt. Ltd, Pondicherry

Printed and bound in Great Britain by Clays Ltd, Elcograf S.p.A.

MIX
Paper from
responsible sources
FSC
www.fsc.org   FSC® C018179

Penguin Random House is committed to a
sustainable future for our business, our readers
and our planet. This book is made from Forest
Stewardship Council® certified paper.

To all my family.
How fortunate I am to have them.

Contents

Introduction

According to my calculations (which are unreliable), I have now published eighteen books, so I have written a lot of introductions and probably told people as much about me as anyone would reasonably want to know. Certain questions are often repeated though, so I'll answer them in this introduction, in case anyone is still curious.

I was born in Stanford in the Vale, then in Berkshire but now in Oxfordshire, since the unfortunate shifting of the historic county boundaries. I lived in the village until I was eighteen, and growing up in that region, in one of the beautiful isolated villages in the shallow valley below the Uffington White Horse, I spoke with the strong dialect of the area. I did not realise this at the time because everyone I knew spoke in the same way, and it was only when I left home and people started to fall about laughing that I realised my speech was different to that of anyone else.

I am the youngest of six children and have four brothers and a sister. Our dad, Stanley Ayres, served in the Grenadier Guards and held them in great esteem. He was in active service all through the Second World War and spent long harrowing periods in Caen and Falaise in the period following D-Day. Afterwards he worked for the Southern Electricity Board as a linesman, channelling electricity or 'the juice' out to where it was needed and climbing the tarry poles in spiked boots. In the foulest of weather those men went out in teams to deal with breaks in the power caused by lightning strikes, storm damage and collisions with big birds like swans. He was tough. He was the toughest man I ever knew.

I loved writing as soon as I could do it. Wonderful teachers stand out to me as I look back. Bill Reeves and Mr Holifield at Faringdon Secondary Modern School where I went after I failed the eleven-plus. They were brilliant and encouraged me to write. Mr Reeves gave me a special book in which to pen my stories and Mr Holifield had me contributing yarns for the modest school newspaper grandly entitled the *Conquest*. Those things matter. They give a child confidence in their abilities. I remember those teachers, and others, with gratitude.

It was my great good fortune that not only did I love writing, I also loved performing, so that when I had written something I wanted to be the one to get up on stage and put it across. I didn't like hearing someone else trying to perform my work. I wanted to get them by the throat and shout, 'You're saying it *all WRONG!*' Almost everything I write is for performance. I don't write much that is to be read to oneself in silence in a leafy glade.

I live my life in the hope of coming up with good ideas. Of finding myself in a situation, of reading an article, of overhearing a fragment of conversation which sparks off the magic feeling: *That's a good idea! I could do something with that!* I felt it when I was droning round and round the car park in Cirencester looking for a non-existent space, getting later and later for an appointment I didn't want to miss. I felt it as my heart sank when I read in a newspaper article that the formal dinner party was making a comeback. It's a great feeling because I think, 'If this is affecting me, it probably affects everyone else. With a bit of luck I could write something we all identify with.' Having settled on a subject then, I try to think of various ways to approach it, using different angles and not saying the same thing twice. It needs to be just the right length, because nothing kills a comic poem more quickly than being too long. It has to say what needs to be said in as few well-chosen words as possible. Sharp and to the point.

Many, many people write poetry and would like to have it published. I am not keen on the idea of paying publishers. I have always believed that if your work was saleable then the publisher should pay you, but of course it is a personal choice. I do earnestly think that if you believe in your work and know it to have merit, then you shouldn't let it languish in a drawer. You should get it out into the public domain. Perform it, no matter how terrified you may be, because the next time you won't be quite so terrified. I have found it so true that the more you do it, the more you *can* do it. I was paralysed with fear the first few times I stood up and performed my work, but I saw the audience throw itself forward in great tumultuous laughs *at something I had devised, something entirely out of my own brain!* I heard the applause, felt the affection and left the stage dazed by how marvellous it was.

It's a drug of course, this performing. You can never come off it. It doesn't take long to get hooked.

Thank you to everyone who has ever bought a book of mine. Thank you for enabling me to live my life as a writer, when so many people with equal abilities never get the chance.

Pam Ayres, July 2019

Up in the Attic

I've got to find a document, whereabouts unknown,
I haven't seen the thing since George VI was on the
    throne,
A copy's unacceptable, or so the jobsworth said,
There's only one place left to look, and that's the
    one I dread.
It isn't in the chest with the drawers stuffed full,
It isn't in the cupboard with the old knitting wool,
It isn't in the garden where the cauliflowers grow,
Where is it? Where *is* it? I think we all know ...

It's up in the attic, where the wind blows chill,
Up in the attic where the woodworm drill,
Up in the attic with the dust and the fluff,
Up in the attic with a load of other stuff.
Up the shaky ladder to the hole as black as pitch,
Up the shaky apparatus feeling for the switch,
Up to the attic where the temperature drops,
Up in the attic where the friendliness stops.

Here's the little table where the clock used to stand,
Here's a photograph of Granny changing on the
    sand,
That photograph you took on holiday in
    Perranporth,
When a cold wave slapped her, and her teeth shot
    forth.

Up in the attic there's a big old clock,
A big old rocking horse that's never going to rock,
A farm and a castle and a little Noah's Ark,
And a doll's house, beautiful, but all the rooms are
    dark.

A doll's house, beautiful, palatial in its day,
Closed up now, the occupants have gone away,
Gone with the passengers waiting for the train,
Here on a set that'll never run again.
There's a box with a wedding dress straight from
    the bride,
The body of a little mouse. Mummified.
A disappointed spider on the cobwebbed floor,
He hasn't caught a fly since the Second World War.

There's a big old bumblebee lying on her back,
Built for the summer sun; trapped in the black,
No flower can anticipate a visit from her,
For the dust lies thick on her black-and-yellow fur.
Oh, *where* is the document? Where's it been shoved?
At the back of all the bric-a-brac no one ever loved?
In the Christmas decorations? By the half-lagged
    tank?
Where the dead birds wallowed and the ballcock sank.

There's insurance certificates relating to the house,
A last will and testament to benefit the spouse.
All the vital documents that punctuate your life,
Little kiddies' works-of-art that cut you like a knife,
A drop-side cot in a shade of baby blue,
The paint's gnawed off, but it's still as good as new,
And this'll show you what a sentimentalist I am –
Together with the parasol: my children's ancient
    pram.

Here in the flicker of the solitary light,
Here all the memories still shine bright,
Cold through a crack, comes the glimmer of the
    moon,
Shining on a lifetime, flown too soon.
All this stuff wants taking up the tip!
All this stuff wants putting in the skip!
All this forgotten clutter, sorrowful and brown ...
I'll leave it for the kids when I'm six feet down.

When I was a young woman, I was desperate to travel. I would have gone anywhere; I longed to discover and experience as many other countries as possible.

As it turned out, I was fortunate. I travelled a great deal and loved it, so that I no longer feel that desperation. These days, if you asked me to describe my perfect day out, it probably wouldn't involve hopping on an aeroplane at all. I think I'd choose a nice walk on a Sunday in spring and then a pub lunch. A picturesque pub please, and a nice corner table by the fire. I'd take a heap of Sunday newspapers, and for company I would like my husband Dudley and our dog. I would be ecstatically happy. Well, until a year or two ago I would have been. But nowadays, the pubs have started to do something I don't like ...

Don't Put My Dinner on the Slate

When I fancy fish and chips and wander down the
     pub,
Please don't put a roofing slate underneath my grub.
Call me out of fashion, call me old and out of date,
But when it comes to cod and chips, I want it on
     a plate.

Serve it on a breadboard and the smile dies on my
     lips,
I imagine other diners' curry sauce and chips,
Lurking in the crevices and hiding in the cracks,
So please, remove the board and set about it with
     an axe.

Plates are very useful, they have stood the test of
     time,
Their surfaces are highly glazed for shrugging off
     the grime,
Who then was the genius, the one who introduced,
Surfaces which cannot be fastidiously sluiced?

Just a simple plate would do, something you can
  wash,
Not the Royal Worcester or the Villeroy & Boch,
Not the finest china with a willow pattern scene,
Something ordinary. Something boring. Something
  clean!

Caterers and chefs, if you would like my grateful
  thanks,
Please don't put my fish and chips on slates and tiles
  and planks,
Though not on the menu with lasagne and paella,
I'm afraid I might have paid for added salmonella.

I read a disturbing newspaper article recently. It announced that the formal dinner party was making a comeback. The casual friendliness of the kitchen supper was long gone, said the pundit, and once again the stiff ritual of the formal dinner party would be the only socially acceptable form of entertaining.

'What baloney!' I thought with scorn. As if anybody would willingly return to those evenings and the monumental amount of work they involved. My early, fearful attempts at proper dinner parties scarred me for life. I soon gave up, leaving a trail of woody parsnips, still-raw apple crumbles and atrociously cooked meats behind me.

I used to work beside a fearful snob of a woman. She had married money and now spoke with an affected, upper-crust accent:

'Ai had a lovely dinner party on Saturday evenin'. Duck à l'orange and all the trimmin's, we 'ad.'

I used to say, 'Oh, lovely,' while reflecting that I myself had enjoyed baked beans straight out of the saucepan.

No, *dinner parties can make a comeback for somebody else. I'm not getting involved.*

The Dinner Party

It seemed like such a good idea, a flash of
  inspiration,
To hold a dinner party! Yes, out went the invitations,
A proper dinner party too, traditional and smart,
With all my oldest, dearest friends, the darlings of
  my heart.

We'd clear the dining table of each dog-eared magazine,
We'd dust around the skirting boards, the place
  would be pristine,
We'd pick up all the clutter, drive the hoover round
  the floor,
And see again our carpet after eighteen months
  or more.

I'd plan a lovely menu, seven courses at the least,
An absolute abundance, an ambrosia, a feast!
With table linen matching and the candles burning
  bright,
What a celebration! What a banquet! What a night!

Yeah. Well.

That was then and this is now, and one thing's very
    clear,
I can't imagine why I thought this was a good idea,
Today's the day, tonight's the night, they'll be here
    in an hour,
I'm absolutely shattered, and I haven't had a shower.

I haven't chilled the wine or put the nibbles in a
    bowl,
I found my silver cutlery, it's all as black as coal,
I haven't found the candles, we are making do with
    these,
One's a stump and one is bent at forty-five degrees.

I haven't folded napkins in sophisticated shapes,
Or beautified a plate of cheese with celery and
    grapes,
I haven't spent the morning on a floral centrepiece,
And I'm skidding round the kitchen floor on half an
    inch of grease.

My husband's disappeared, I don't know where he's
    hiding now,
He hasn't helped *at all*, we've had a monumental
    row,
I don't know where the day is gone, and I am filled
    with dread,
Forget the conversation, I just want to go to bed.

The guests I thought were witty, their attractiveness
    has palled,
The men, once so enticing, now they're boring and
    they're bald,
The women all are shadows of their former vibrant
    selves,
They're all in sizes twenty-four, they used to be
    in twelves.

I stupidly asked George, I used to think him quite a
    card,
Not meaning to be spiteful, now he's just a tub
    of lard,
He'll bring his lovely wife, she'll tell you all about
    her back,
One's morbidly obese and ones a hypochondriac.

I haven't found the coffee cups, we'll have to have
the mugs,
The crumble's looking soggy and the kale was full
of slugs,
The meat is a disaster, undercooked and full of
blood,
The dog's pooed on the carpet and I haven't done
the spuds.

I thought I'd like to do this, but I don't know where
to start,
I thought I'd like to see them, but I've had a change
of heart,
Their old recycled stories and voracious appetites,
Forget the darlings of my heart, they're all a bunch
of shites.

I meant to be the glam hostess but kiss goodbye to
that,
I haven't changed my frock, I smell attractively of fat,
I've done my best, it's all gone west, I've ruined all
the grub,
Too late. Here come the bastards now. Let's all go
down the pub.

Puppies in Their Basket

Puppies in their basket,
Smell as sweet as any roses.
Older doggies smell,
Of flatulence and halitosis.

The Dog Who Bit the Ball

I am the dog who bit the ball,
And ruined the game of goals.
I wasn't to know, that balls don't go,
If you've added a couple of holes.
The kids and dad, they all went mad,
They sent me indoors, they did,
The ball was new, a beautiful blue,
And it cost them several quid.

The shame, the shame, I ruined the game.
And made the family crabby,
I jumped for it, I shook it a bit,
And it went from hard to flabby,
'Bad dog!' they said, 'Go in your bed!'
And in disgrace I go,
I offered a paw, but nobody saw,
Nobody wanted to know.

Here comes the boss, she's ever so cross,
Her face is black as thunder,
I'm in my bed, expression of dread,
My tail tucked down and under,
With hands on hips and scold on lips,
She tells me I'm a *menace*,
I'm finding it tough, this football stuff,
Anyone care for tennis?

The rule, you see, for dogs like me,
Is simple, I'll recite it:
Don't kick a ball for terriers small,
And think that they won't bite it.
I'm not too grand to lick her hand,
I sidle up and risk it ...
I think I've won ... look, everyone!
She's gone to get a biscuit!

Banging

The builders are busy at our house,
With a portable loo standing near,
Hard the wind blows,
And the door doesn't close,
Brother, it's banging round here.

O ur dad, Stanley Ayres, had a good turn of phrase. He could really make me laugh. Conversely, he could soon cut you down to size if he thought you hadn't done your best, or had gone about a job in a thoughtless, slapdash fashion. Then, he would look at the scene disparagingly and say, 'Pitiful. 'Tis pitiful. You might as well have left the job alone.' I hated it when he said that; when you didn't get his approval and he dismissed your efforts. Mind you, it hasn't stopped me aiming the same observation at my poor long-suffering husband. Particularly when he sees himself in the role of handyman ...

Pitiful

Now, my man is very clever,
With his spreadsheets and whatever,
But I wish he wouldn't tackle DIY.
For our draught-excluded door,
Doesn't open any more,
And honestly? I wish he wouldn't try.

Hanging pictures on the wall,
Is that difficult, at all?
Surely there's a way if there's a will,
But I began to fear the worst,
When I heard the picture cursed,
And the dropping of the Black & Decker drill.

Oh, it's pitiful, pitiful, absolutely pitiful,
The most pathetic thing you've ever known,
What a failure, what a dud,
Here's a bucket for the blood,
He might as well have left the job alone.

The loo, it wasn't flushing,
It was gurgling and gushing,
And the situation soon was as I feared:
He said, 'I'll have a go!'
And I thought: 'Oh God, oh no!'
As carrying a spanner, he appeared.

I was watching what he did:
Lifting off the cistern lid,
He identified a problem with the flow,
Well, he faddled and he fiddled,
And he daddled and he diddled,
Then he straightened up and said he didn't know.

Oh, it's pitiful, pitiful, absolutely pitiful,
The most pathetic thing you've ever known,
A catastrophe, a bummer,
Should have gone and got a plumber,
He might as well have left the job alone.

The bathroom isn't nice,
You wouldn't want to visit twice,
It is out of date, unwelcoming and cold.
The basin has a crack,
It's been leaking down the back,
Redolent of mildew and of mould.

I was overcome with doubt,
When I saw him get the grout,
And he said, 'We needn't suffer any more!'
Though its beauty never hit you,
Still the basin was in situ,
Now it lies in pieces on the floor.

Oh, it's pitiful, pitiful, absolutely pitiful,
The most pathetic thing you've ever known,
What we should have done (I knew it),
Was *get someone in* to do it.
He might as well have left the job alone.

It is true that I am vexed,
I don't know what he'll ruin next,
And his ladder looks a little bit unsteady.
In just putting up a shelf,
He can electrocute himself,
So have the ambulances standing ready.

Homebase and Wickes he visits,
With his checklist of requisites,
And I'm not a person effortlessly irked,
But the cash for all this gear,
Would pay a tradesman for a year,
And, in the end, we'd have a thing that worked.

Oh, it's pitiful, pitiful, absolutely pitiful,
The most pathetic thing you've ever known,
A conundrum to bewilder:
Why I didn't wed a builder,
I might as well have left the job alone.

Loss of the Lego

Alas! We've lost the last piece of the Lego,
And have no hope of finishing our truck,
One flick, and the last brick of the Lego,
Has gone! We can't believe our rotten luck.

Our lorry cannot reach its destination,
But our misfortune doesn't stop at that,
For in a moment of miscalculation,
We fear it has been eaten by the cat.

It wouldn't do to persecute the tabby,
His eyes are dimmer now than once they were,
His quest is to digest his prey of plastic,
While wondering why it hasn't any fur.

We cannot now affix our radiator,
Which means our truck will surely overheat,
Imagine the response of Health and Safety,
At boiling water round our driver's feet ...

Abandoning our task in grief and sorrow,
I'll do what all the other grannies did,
Take along my disappointed grandchild,
And buy another set for forty quid.

Kiwi Fruit

I purchased a kiwi marked 'Perfectly Ripe',
Well! What baloney, what rubbish, what tripe!
On taking a bite from it, oh, what a shock,
The 'succulent' fruit was as hard as a rock!

You labouring labellers, hidden from view,
Your claims are preposterous, false and untrue,
The food-buying public is vocal: it speaks!
This here kiwi fruit needs another three weeks!

Geriatric Juliet

The smell of Pot Noodles is rank round the place,
While on an increasingly elderly face,
I slap on the slap, and though once I was glam,
Nowadays nobody knows who I am.

I get no auditions for Shakespeare or farce,
Jobs, like my eyelashes, daily grow sparse,
The radiant smile which struck men with such force,
Has started to look rather more like a horse.

When I walk on the stage, no one's heart skips a beat,
It's hard on your knees and it's hard on your feet,
Dressing Room One, I'd invariably have,
But now I'm in Nine, by the side of the lav.

This once was my empire with flowers bedecked,
With laughter, champagne, admiration unchecked,
Warmth and excitement, we flirted and laughed.
But times have grown cold. I am feeling the draught.

My beautiful talented friends of the day,
Their faces have dimmed, they have melted away,
They took a last bow, disappeared from the stage,
In retirement homes they succumb to their age.

The days I played Juliet, how they have flown,
And Romeo's past it, no joints are his own,
Nothing is left of us, nothing at all,
And even the balcony fell off the wall.

I never foresaw, at the height of my fame,
'Veteran Actress' alongside my name,
I never envisioned the people who said:
'Yeah, I remember her; thought she was dead.'

Farewell thrown flowers and standing ovation,
To newer performers there's been a migration,
Thus to an end my soliloquy draws,
Bring down the curtain; cue scattered applause.

*L*ike innumerable other people, I felt I had an idea for a stage musical. Having worked as a guest speaker on several cruise ships, I chose one of them as my setting, because I had been struck by the difference between conditions up on the smart passenger decks compared with those on the cramped, utilitarian crew decks lower down.

In this scene the crew are truly fed up with the 'them and us' situation. They are each clutching a teddy bear, standing by their bunks, and singing this song. It is harmonised in the style of a Welsh male voice choir.

Stop me in the street, I'll sing it for you.

All So Different Down Below

Oh, it's all so different down below,
Here, where the punters never go,
Where our boots ring on the steel,
Down beside the mighty keel,
No shagpile, no plush,
Nothing sumptuous or lush.
The wide Sargasso Sea,
Is no place for him and me,
For its all so different down below.

Oh Lord, as I'm lying on my bunk,
Never let my mother see how low I've sunk,
For with cruising we are *bored*,
We've sailed up every bloody fjord,
To earn our daily bread,
We go round and *round* the Med,
Oh Lord, won't you give us,
Something else to do instead,
For it's all so different down below.

They are dining underneath the chandelier,
Here, conditions are a little more austere,
Here the strip lights harshly glare,
And we want to be up there,
On this, the queen of ships,
How come we're eating chips?
They've lobster thermidor,
But they are rich, and we are poor,
And it's all so different down below.

Every gentleman's resplendent in his tux,
It makes us gnash our teeth and murmur 'shucks',
We could pose and cut a dash,
If we only had the cash,
Drink champagne and bray,
And frolic in the spray,
We could be adroit,
At the tossing of the quoit,
But it's all so different down below.

We have docked in every single port of call,
But you seen one tourist trap, you seen them all,
There's nothing left on ship or shore,
That we can bother to explore,
One more Arctic moon,
Would be too bloody soon,
We're homesick and we're glum,
And we wish we hadn't come,
For it's all so different down below.

Etna and Stromboli

I was skinny when I boarded but am now quite
    roly-poly,
I've seen the great volcanic sights of Etna and
    Stromboli,
I've seen the glory that was Rome, the birthplace
    of a nation,
And transited the Suez to expand my education.

I've sailed upon a dhow, enjoyed my first taste
    of wasabi,
Saw visual feasts: the Middle East, Qatar and
    Abu Dhabi,
Viewed the Colosseum and the place they made
    papyrus,
Had Clostr'um difficile, E. coli, gyp and
    norovirus.

The Jolly Fishcake

I bought a jolly fishcake,
To have for supper later,
What it lacked in haddock,
It made up for in tater.

Dance Like Your Feet Don't Hurt

Men once adored me, but now they are curt,
I'm severed in half by the waist of my skirt,
Unspeakable ailments are dragging me down,
But yes! YES! To a night on the town!

My once-jolly girlfriends are widowed and bleak,
Stuck in a home at two thousand a week,
In floral armchairs at the end of the journey,
Having relinquished their power of attorney.

Though my generation is ailing or dead,
Though I hear mortality's whisper-soft tread,
I'll laugh, laugh, like I heard what they said,
And dance like my feet don't hurt.

Wide, Baby, Wide

Once in my stiletto heels, I tottered,
Down the old King's Road, I used to stride,
Nowadays I'm in the local Hotter,
Saying, 'I need 'em wide, baby, wide.'

Once in the optician's shop, I pondered,
Which high-fashion lenses should I pick?
Now I don't want tinted or reflective,
Now I need 'em thick, baby, thick.

Once, like perfect pearls, my teeth would sparkle,
Smiling, as you held me in a waltz,
Nowadays you'll find me at the dentist,
Saying, 'I need 'em false, baby, false!'

Remember what you whispered in the darkness?
Suggestive little things that weren't allowed?
Well, now you'd need a good imagination,
And you'd have to say 'em loud, baby, loud.

I can remember the exact moment when I realised that people no longer viewed me as a young woman.

My husband Dudley and I were going out to a posh do and I needed a long dress. At that time, near my home in Cirencester, there was a clothes shop owned and run by an American woman who was brilliant. You could always find something different and original there; she had nothing run-of-the-mill. I walked in and saw this beautiful tangerine-coloured dress hanging up. I tried it on and was filled with a sense of relief and joy. It was perfect! I turned this way and that in front of the mirror: what a stroke of luck! To find something so special so soon! What a fit! And in my favourite colour too! I was busy admiring myself, thinking, 'What a rare beauty! What a looker!'

After a time, the American owner walked over to me. I thought she was going to say something flattering and saleslady-like: that I looked stunning, a vision, the dress could have been made for me – that sort of thing. Instead, she looked me up and down kindly and said, 'Yes … I do think that is rather a tiring style, for the older woman.'

What? You talking about me? Me? Indignation flashed up, but then, when I looked in the mirror again, I realised that I was having to hold everything in to look that skinny. She was absolutely right. It was a beautiful dress, but I was too old for it. It belonged on somebody of eighteen.

So now I think all you can do is adopt an attitude of cheerful resignation to the inevitable decline …

The Next Big Thing

Bring ruddy great frocks, and trousers, and smocks,
Bring all of the latest apparel,
But don't bring 'em skinny, or thinny, or mini,
Bring 'em as big as a barrel,
And sew in a length of industrial strength,
Elastic or plastic or rubber,
Of massive endurance, to give reassurance,
When fighting to hold in the blubber.

Let's not do things by halves! Boots with ruddy
   great calves,
With gussets, elastic, a-straining,
Not sixes or sevens, bring tens or elevens!
Or twelves, if there's any remaining.
Bring a nightdress for me, like a darned great
   marquee,
With flounces and colourful threading,
For a moderate rent, I could hire out my tent,
For parties, bar mitzvahs and weddings.

I'll be free, debonair, I'll buy new underwear,
Away with those bras uninspiring!
No more to entomb the majestic bozoom,
With their cut-you-in-half underwiring,
And as for the panties, I don't want them scanty,
I don't want them frilly or lacy,
Bring 'em big and not sparse, for the *serious* arse,
Who said size twenty-two can't be racy?

Round and Round the Car Park

Round and round the car park, verging on despair,
Round and round the car park, tearing out my hair,
Up and down, round and round, anguish on the face,
Round and round the car park, trying to find a place.

I'm ever so late, I'm ever so late, the whole day's gone
    to pot,
I'm whimpering round the car park, trying to find
    a spot,
Why didn't I get here earlier? I'm thinking more
    and more,
To park your car successfully: start the night before.

I see a shopping couple: they are laden down and hot,
'Excuse me, are you leaving now?' 'No, we're bloody
    not!'
A builder in a Transit van, he might be moving soon
    . . .
No, he's got a burger, he'll be there all afternoon.

There's four behind, and four before, and four more
  join the chain,
Round we go, and down we go, and up we go again,
A man we see, he dangles a key! We're off in hot
  pursuit!
Our hopes are dashed, he's only stashed a parcel in
  the boot.

And that's not fair, see that man there? Reclining,
  having a nap!
Look at him snore in his 4 x 4, down over his eyes:
  a cap!
It makes me blind with anger, I feel fury I can't stop!
I feel like driving into him. (Seems a bit over the top.)

Now tempers flare: 'Don't you go there! *I'm* waiting
  for that space!'
A man bawls from the window with a snarl upon
  his face,
It's feeling like a war zone, it is violent and sour,
Up and down the tarmac for three quarters of an hour.

I'm going home, I'm going home, I know when I'm
  defeated,
I've heard enough abusive stuff you wouldn't want
  repeated,
I'm on my way, goodbye, good day, the situation's gory,
Perhaps I'll try again when they have built a
  multistorey.

Framed

Sell the car! Take out a second mortgage!
Hand me all your jewellery as well!
Cash in our investments, call the broker,
Tell the man to sell, sell, sell!
Now is not the time to be faint-hearted,
Pawn the baby's bangle, old and rare,
Because I stood upon my varifocals,
And somehow must afford another pair.

Even now it's painful to remember,
That Sunday at the sunny picnic lunch,
I stood to pass the coronation chicken,
Took a backward step and heard the crunch.
I stared down at the broken-up components,
The tortoiseshell, the hinges and the frame,
Realising in that very instant,
Our ISA, it would never look the same.

The salesman, he was absolutely charming,
His helpfulness and patience knew no bounds,
Yes, they had a basic varifocal,
Very keenly priced at fifty pounds!
Though there *were* other options to consider:
Did I like designer frames? I did!
And thin? And anti-glare? And non-reflective?
'Right,' he said, 'that's seven hundred quid.'

Stupefied, I fell towards the carpet,
My body he was very swift to catch,
And he whispered in a manner reassuring:
'Eight hundred if you want them anti-scratch.'
These are my brand-new replacement glasses,
Though I'm grateful I no longer have to squint,
Clearly on the banking screen before me,
I can see we're absolutely skint.

Toddlers, newborn babies, little children,
Choose your own career with utmost care,
And if 'optometrist' should be top of your list,
One day you could be a millionaire.

Granny Got Whiskers

Flirtatious glances cannot flick,
Through spectacles with lenses thick.
From dewy skin that plumply shone,
All youthful bloom is lost and gone.
I'm standing up on joints that creak,
With liver spots on hand and cheek,
And in the mirror, Time – the knave –
Has made me think I ought to shave.

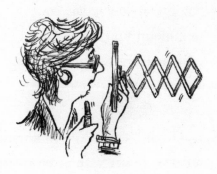

Coshed at the Cashpoint

My granny was coshed at the cashpoint!
She had only just entered her pin,
When out came the dosh,
And down came the cosh!
But Gran, not a gal to give in ...

Turned round and *kneed* her attacker,
Saying, 'Buster, you're making me nervous!'
The machine on the wall,
Having witnessed it all,
Said: 'Thank you for using our service.'

The Toff at the Top

Oh, let me be ruled by an Eton-schooled,
Patrician kind of fellow,
A rowing type, of a military stripe,
With a wife who plays the cello,
Who rides to hounds through wooded grounds,
And haunts the Highlands lonely,
To stalk the crag, with gralloched stag,
Across the ghillie's pony.

In robust health on the Glorious Twelfth,
He's off to bag the birdies,
In a heathered butt with one eye shut,
And a matching pair of Purdeys,
And a twenty-bore on the purple moor,
And the thrill of the driven grouse,
Then wine and dine and sleep supine,
In a chum's baronial house.

The cream of the crop, the toff at the top,
The soft manipulators,
A benevolent smile, a stately pile,
And plenty of rolling acres,
Where sculpted busts of the upper crust,
Embellish the marble halls,
With flaming logs and working dogs,
And thoroughbreds in the stalls.

Capability Brown, a place in town,
Hurrah for the ruling classes.
The noble bones and imperious tones,
Of numberless cut-glasses.
Who can compete? Not the man in the street,
Who hasn't the lands extensive,
Who wants to be led by poor old Fred,
The cream of the comprehensive?

It does not lie, the old school tie,
The voice refined and cool,
For vowels precise, they come at a price,
When they come from a public school,
So lead on sire! Though life be dire,
Unswerving loyalty,
Will drive us on, though hope be gone,
It's a toff at the top for me.

*A*t eighteen years of age, bored beyond endurance by my form-filling job in the civil service, I joined the WRAF as a not-very-good plotter of aerial photography. At nineteen, to my delight and disbelief, I was posted to RAF Seletar in Singapore. This was a coveted posting, which made me the envy of my friends.

I was a village girl. Up to that point, the furthest I had strayed from my Berkshire home was Butlin's in Skegness. The prospect of flying thousands of miles to the other side of the globe filled me with indescribable excitement and joy. The day came. My brother Tony took me to Gatwick airport, and Mum came as well to see me off.

The aircraft was a British Eagle Britannia and the flight took twenty-seven hours, stopping at Kuwait and Colombo in what was then Ceylon.

What I remember most is the overwhelming feeling of film-star glamour as I went up the steps to board the aircraft. At the top, it was all I could do not to turn and wave to my non-existent adoring fans. Flying was still a *rare form of travel then, few people experienced it, and yet there I was, by some unimagined combination of events, about to board a real aircraft and fly off to distant, strange and foreign lands, and to live there for two years! It was the most thrilling day of my entire life.*

A couple of years ago, I flew to Sydney with my husband for a friend's wedding. Although I have flown a lot in the intervening years, this time I couldn't help thinking about that first joyous journey. The contrast was stark. All glamour associated with long-haul flights is long gone, replaced by flinty-eyed efficiency and strict security. Airports are vast and jam-packed with people. There is an ever-present wariness, constant warnings about unattended baggage, a low-lying knowledge that this big airport is a target which might be attacked. Passing through Security, you have to take your shoes off and remove your belt. You are sniffed, scanned and herded like cattle. You know it's all necessary, done for your own good, blah-blah, and so you grit your teeth and get on with it. Just join the next queue. Endure the indignity.

We were only in Sydney briefly. We attended the lovely wedding and stayed for a week or so longer. As is usual for me, I felt jetlagged for the first ten days, then, having perked up, I got on the plane, came home and felt jetlagged all over again. So overall, I felt unusually jaded with the whole business of long-haul flights and not keen to do another one any time soon. Out of my dejection, however, came this series of linked poems called 'Flight Time'. It looks at various aspects of a long-haul flight.

Flight Time

Departure

At the airport, running late,
I've never been in such a state,
Which is our departure gate?
It's teeming,
Streaming,
I am close to screaming.

Everywhere a sense of panic,
Asian, African, Hispanic,
Scan the board with eyeballs manic,
Blowing,
Glowing,
Wish I wasn't going.

Passport on the check-in shelf,
'Have you packed this all yourself?'
'No, it was Santa and his elf.'
Never,
Be clever,
No humour whatsoever.

She gestures off, I see the view.
Another endless, shuffling queue.

Security

Security's a glimpse of Hell,
Here's my liquid, here's my gel,
Have my shoes, they're hot, they smell,
Profess them,
Confess them,
Let the man assess them.

Through the scanner you must trot,
Will you ring the bell or not?
Yes – stand aside or else be shot,
They'll search you,
Besmirch you,
On a screen research you.

'Can I touch you?' If you must,
Provided you're devoid of lust,
Come pat me down, come, stroke my bust,
Inspect me,
Protect me,
Don't let the bombs affect me.

Your blue-gloved hands and steely eyes,
Keep me safe while in the skies.

Boarding

Relief! I've found my seat at last,
Tucked away my boarding pass,
Belted up, secure and fast,
So fly me!
Ply me!
Folk are shuffling by me.

On come stags inebriated,
Sobbing grannies separated,
Honeymooners impregnated,
City
Slicker.
Please walk a little quicker.

The captain's speaking from his deck,
'Cabin crew: arm doors, cross check,'
Soon in the sky, we'll be a speck,
Soaring,
Roaring,
Safety talk ignoring.

Recline the seat which does, I find,
Infuriate the bloke behind.

Sleep

The seat belt sign has been switched off,
Bring us alcohol to quaff,
Ready, steady, head in trough,
Wine us,
Dine us,
And at the back malign us.

Thirst is slaked and hunger sated,
Pupils by free beer dilated,
Gut by flatulence inflated,
Swollen,
Colon,
All control, stolen.

On we fly without a glitch,
Through the night as black as pitch,
Cabin warm and methane-rich,
Steward!
Waiter!
Bring a respirator.

Press the flight attendant's bell,
Are they coming? Are they hell.

The Aircraft Toilet

At last, the aircraft toilet's free,
Now everyone can wait for *me*,
The floor's awash, I think it's pee,
It's widdle.
Piddle.
Someone missed the middle.

In the mirror, some old hag,
Don't bother with the make-up bag,
Or think of lighting up a fag,
It's shabby,
I'm crabby,
You couldn't swing a tabby.

Dare I flush? Fight down my fear,
That roar to *shatter* both your ears,
And suck you to the stratosphere,
Reeling,
Squealing,
Clinging to the ceiling.

I hate these squalid aircraft loos,
And wish that I had worn my shoes.

Fear

Relax? Less easy done than said,
In turbulence I'm gripped by dread,
Appalling scenes are in my head,
Of falling,
Calling,
Search vessels trawling.

Don't let imagination race,
Don't hear: 'Brace for impact – BRACE!'
Don't swallow us without a trace,
Blind us,
Grind us,
No one would ever find us.

Flashing light upon the wing,
Seated by the aircraft skin,
Cold as death and paper-thin,
Sit back,
Settle,
In three hundred tons of metal.

How thin the air, how dark the night,
At minus-sixty Fahrenheit.

Landing

Landed now and doors to manual,
Like some droopy-eyed old spaniel,
Scalding lemon-scented flannel,
Bloated,
Dry-throated,
Tongue with fur, coated.

To the upper locker go,
Cabin baggage swinging low,
Concuss the chappie down below,
He's glaring,
I'm raring,
Ready to go haring.

Swiftly down the aircraft aisle,
The baggage hall is half a mile,
Find a trolley, feeling vile,
Weary,
Bleary,
Detest the fellows cheery.

A tumbled mass, a warning bell,
A surge towards the carousel.

Arrival

I'm all stocked up with Duty Free
A walking winery, that's me,
So shattered I can hardly see,
With spirits,
Sloshing,
And case of dirty washing.

I walk through Nothing to Declare,
A single customs man is there,
I'm nearly through, I'm nearly there!
I'm yearning,
He's turning ...
My suitcase he is churning.

Out at last with features sagging,
Puffy ankles, feet are dragging,
Past the chauffeurs, name cards wagging,
Saw me,
Ignored me,
Nobody's waiting for me.

Find the car, drive home half-dead,
Junk mail mountain. Fall on bed.

I was introduced to the notion of a worm farm by a friend in Robe, South Australia. We'd gone round for a barbecue and she was keen to show off her new hobby. The contraption was parked outside the garage and looked for all the world like a stack of lime-green washing-up bowls on little legs. To call it a farm seemed a bit overblown. Whipping off the lid revealed layers of cabbage leaves and, er ... worms. The resultant fluid, having traversed the entire length of the worms' innards, was painstakingly drawn off by a little lime-green tap at the bottom. It is reputed to be both miraculous for the garden and exceedingly stinky.

Worm Farm

Song of the vermiculturist

I had a little worm farm, it caused a lot of rows,
It wasn't like a proper farm, it hadn't any cows,
We shredded up the cabbage, we were worm-
   farm cranks,
And we fed it to the worms, but they never
   said thanks.

A worm's disadvantage is, he won't do what you
    say,
He won't run and fetch a stick, he won't sit and
    stay,
He won't come to greet you with a bark and a
    bound,
Worms are rather limited, they just … lie around.

We bought a proper home, with the bedding and
    the tap,
All delivered to the door by a worm-farm chap,
He gave us our instructions, all the things we had to
    do,
And promised us an avalanche of worm-farm poo.

Now worm-farm poo is a very special thing,
A heroic fertiliser; it'll nourish anything,
It'll glorify the garden and revitalise our pots,
So welcome, little wiggly worms!
                     We hope you've got the trots.

Poor Old Father Christmas

Twenty days to Christmas!
(Adjust the days to suit.)
I hope that Father Christmas,
Will include us on his route,
I hear the sleigh bells jingle,
As into view he hove,
I hope he is petite,
We've got a new woodburning stove.

See the mighty mansion:
The terrace mean and small,
Poor old Father Christmas,
Has to struggle down them all.
Santa and his reindeer,
They soar above the fields,
The poor old boy's exhausted,
And he's only done South Shields.

Console the little children,
Dispel their childish fright,
Of strangers at the bedside,
In the silence of the night.
Keep at it, Father Christmas!
Most stoical of chaps,
Only six more continents,
And then you can collapse.

Alas, Poor Snowman

Alas poor snowman, there he goes,
The grapey eyes, the parsnip nose,
The pigeon-feathered chic beret,
A thaw has come; he cannot stay.

By little ones with frozen hands,
Built and patted, there he stands.
All must perish, all must pass,
A faceless heap upon the grass.

*O*n 19 April 2018, the five-year-old mare Dame Rose collapsed and died at Cheltenham Racecourse, having come fourth over a two-and-a-half-mile hurdle race. It was the hottest April day since 1949. She was one of six horses to die at the Cheltenham Festival that year.

Dame Rose

Pray silence, pray silence, for poor Dame Rose,
Slip the sheepskin noseband down over her nose,
Lay a hand on her flank, she is down, she is done,
Dame Rose is dead in the Cheltenham sun.

Dame Rose was dainty and glossily dark,
Braided and booted and bright as a lark,
Two miles of endeavour and hurdles to clear,
On the hottest unmerciful day of the year.

Bring the tarpaulin now, put up the screen,
The mare Dame Rose is too sad to be seen,
The sweltering heat gave her much to endure,
But poor Dame Rose, she is cool now for sure.

The Fisherman's Dog

I wish my man would start to doubt,
The rectitude of catching trout,
And tire of these conditions dank,
Here, upon the riverbank.

I hope that soon he weary grows,
Of dewdrops dripping from his nose,
And, crouched beneath the brolly's dome,
Starts to think of going home.

I hope his flask runs out of tea,
I hope, for once, he'll notice me,
As my teeth chatter in my jaws,
And I am frozen to the paws.

Beside this cold and wintry stream,
Of my cosy bed I dream,
And hope my owner shortly may,
Give his fishing rod away.

But yet more fishes must he get,
To flounder in his landing net,
Another maggot hooked and white,
As onward, onward comes the night.

I'd love my supper in my bowl,
A blazing fire of logs and coal,
And in the firelight's homely glare,
To sleep with four feet in the air.

The Curse of the Country Walk

What pillock hung the poo bag from the briar?
Leaving this unlovely scene,
Because,
If that's all you can do,
Hang up the doggy poo,
You might as well have left it where it was.

We've always had a dog and, in my experience, they are very good at choosing what they hear. Suppose it was cold and pouring with rain, and you invited our dog out into the garden for a late-night pee, well she might not hear that. Your voice might float unheeded over her sleeping form. On the other hand, if you picked up a crackly packet containing those dog treats that are supposed to clean their teeth, she'd hear that. Even if she was in a distant part of the house with the TV blaring and somebody clog-dancing, she'd be up, ears pricked, and at your side like a shot.

The Crackly Packet

I like the sound of a crackly packet,
Containing my favourite treat,
My human normally buys them,
From the shop at the end of our street.
They live in the crackly packet abode,
And my human's usual ploy,
Is to give me a treat from the crackly packet,
Whenever I've been a good boy.

When feeling the lack of a crackly packet,
You have to pull out all the stops,
Must be a good chap, jump up on her lap,
And give her a lick round the chops.
You can't declare war on the black Labrador,
When the thought of a tasty treat hits you,
You can't have a spat with the neighbouring cat,
Or jump on the back of the shih-tzu.

Humans are straightforward creatures,
They're partial to boxes of chocs,
And don't in the least like a carcase, deceased,
Or a roll in the poo of a fox ...
They fiddle about, with a kiss on the snout,
And affectionate cup of the muzzle,
They twiddle your ear, though you're making it clear,
That you only want something to guzzle.

Can't talk any more! She's just walked in the door ...
Her steely resolve, can I crack it?
I'm looking adoring ... devoted ... imploring,
Yessss! Here comes the crackly packet!

Stairlift Song

Once the night-time was laden with passion,
And the mattress with lust was aflame ...
But now, 'Shall we summon the stairlift?'
Somehow doesn't feel quite the same.

Unfinished

Have you seen these little bootees that I'm making
   for my son?
I've finished one completely, now I'm on the second
   one,
I'm knitting them myself, they've not been made by
   a machine!
Only now my son is thirty;
And his feet are size fourteen.

Have you seen this lovely tapestry I'm working on
   of late?
I'm going to make a screen to hide the black and
   empty grate,
The picture's of a village green, a duck pond and
   a spire,
Only lately we've downsized;
Our new house hasn't got a fire.

And what about this lovely dress I'm making for
    myself?
(I find it very difficult to buy them off the shelf.)
The fabric is luxurious, a banquet for the eyes!
But it looks old-fashioned now;
And, anyway, I'm twice the size.

But one day I shall finish them! And then I'll start
    some more,
With pride and satisfaction, I'll show off the empty
    drawer,
I'll finish my creations and display them with
    pizzazz!
If it takes me *twenty years*!
Oh. It already has.

Until I Hear the News

I'm such a happy person and my smile is like the
    sun,
I greet my fellow humans, and I love them, every
    one,
My joy lights up the firmament, I never get the
    blues,
I'm bouncing with the thrill of life. Until I watch
    the news.
And then, into my home, there bursts a barren
    battle scene,
The homeless and the stricken and the suffering
    obscene,
A wasteland of atrocities, of bleakness and of dread,
And I think I'll get a noose and hang myself out in
    the shed.

The sun is on the dewy grass, I'm walking with
   my dog,
The robin he is singing, on a lichen-covered log,
A Sunday paper, raggedly, is blown across the park,
I idly scan the headlines, and I feel my day grow dark.
The earthquake and the avalanche, the famine and
   the flood,
Barbarity unspeakable, the carnage and the blood,
The bomber and the slasher, the disaster in the skies,
And I think I'll get a gun and shoot myself between
   the eyes.

I'm lying on the beach, the sun is warm upon
   my limbs,
I've got a crispy salad and a fruity glass of Pimm's,
The little waves are lapping, I'm enchanted by
   the views,
But someone has a radio; we listen to the news.
Our kids are building castles, playing happy splashy
   games,
While other children scatter from their villages
   in flames,
Little ones, defenceless and an unresisting prey,
Waiting for salvation. And it isn't on its way.

Perhaps I'll be a hermit, live a life of solitude,
I'd build myself a shelter and have centipedes
   for food,
A shack, deep in the forest, with a cosy compost loo,
Wherein no news presenter ever comes to spoil
   the view.
There I'd play my old guitar in blissful isolation,
Endeavouring to never get a scrap of information,
Keep a little goat and honeybees in wooden hives,
Try not to think of other people's bloody awful lives.

You give your cash to charity, you try to do your bit,
But hard to be undaunted by the utter scale of it,
Half the world is wealthy, through their lucky lives
   may dance,
Half the world is desperate and doesn't get a chance.
It's all too much for me, so let the end be kind
   and quick,
A friendly cannonball or else a swig of arsenic,
Or leaping from a clifftop with a last despairing howl,
So all the world will know that I am throwing in
   the towel.

Once-Topical Tweets

No. 1: Moving to the Moon

I think I'll live upon the moon,
For Putin, Trump and Kim Jong-un,
Have made me view the months ahead,
With trepidation, fear and dread.

I need to travel up there quick,
I'll have a word with Branson, Dick,
Afford the fare, get in, escape,
And gaze down from my lunarscape.

Beside some crater I will go,
View the apocalypse below,
And feel inestimably sad;
We did not value what we had.

No. 2: The Bodyguard

I wish I had a bodyguard to keep me safe from harm,
A manly sort of geezer with a gritty sort of charm,
To stand alert and ready in the corridors of power,
And drive the limo backwards at a hundred miles
   an hour.

A bodyguard, a bodyguard, my foes to scrutinise,
And if they look suspicious, shoot 'em straight between
   the eyes,
Protect me from the terrorist, the footstep close behind,
And give a gal some lovin' when her husband's disinclined.

No. 3: Mrs May's Hair

One thing I do admire in Mrs May:
She's not afraid to let her hair go grey.
No dye from pricey crimpers does she seek,
To keep the fabled barnet looking chic.

Unlike us timid ones, who monthly go,
To cover up the roots as white as snow,
And, in our fight to look less like an Alp,
Endure the fiery tint upon the scalp.

We, who pay a fortune as we leave,
Remember Mrs May, and softly grieve,
Though some may choose to take the cheaper path,
And do the job themselves, over the bath.

No. 4: Trump's Anatomy

On meeting Mr President,
Poor Mrs May must quake,
Which part of her anatomy,
Will he decide to shake?

No. 5: Salisbury

I went down to Salisbury,
To listen to the choir,
A pair of Russian tourists there,
Were staring up the spire,
Staring up the spire they were,
Silent and aghast:
Against the sky, hurtling by:
A piggy flying past!

No. 6: A Wish for Archie

I wish you, little baby Archie,
Jolly times, not stiff and starchy,
A happy life, with Mum and Dad,
Kinder than your father had.

*I*t seems to me that people spend a lot of time putting together eulogies to be read out at funerals. They take much time and trouble choosing exactly the right words to describe what a person meant to them, to list their fine qualities and character and their many kindnesses. This is all admirable, except that the person upon whom the praise is being heaped never gets to hear it. They never learn how important and loved they were in life, or how they massively enhanced the lives of others.

Well I'm not having any truck with all that. This is a poem for my sister Jean, without whom my life would be thin indeed. While we are both still going strong, I want her to know how much I love her. I am glad to have lived my life beside her. She is the best sister I could possibly have had.

I hope I can always find her.

Jean's Poem

For a sister

I don't know if there is a Heaven,
With green meadows and woods,
Banks studded with primroses,
The sound of water trickling on mossy stones,
And things of great beauty.
Ferns frozen within icicles,
The harebell, the sun on the sea,
A snugly wrapped baby,
A puppy dog.

I don't know if there is a place,
Where animals are treated kindly at last,
Where there is love and light, as we read in our
    holy books,
Where we may sit at God's right hand,
Be judged pound for pound, good for bad,
Where angels sing.

Up there in the clouds somewhere,
In some other sphere, another realm.
After we are gone from our homes.
Gone away. Died on such-and-such a date.

But I know this:
You were crucial to me all my life.
You made the dark times more bearable,
The bright days brighter;
Punctuated the years with warmth and colour.
And knowing that you loved me with all my flaws,
I was strengthened and comforted.
And after we have gone,
Wherever we are, whatever we shall be,
I will come looking for you,
And you come looking for me.

I was born after the end of the Second World War, but national service continued until 1960, when the last young men were called up to do their compulsory eighteen-month stint in the armed forces.

Three of my four brothers had to enlist and so did the brothers of all my friends. Men in uniform were a common sight everywhere. They travelled to and from their barracks by train, using railway warrants issued by the forces. The stations were often thronged with soldiers. Hardly anybody had a car.

My uncle Sam, scrupulously smart in his black uniform, worked at our local railway station at Challow, and my mother visited her brother there often. We propped our bikes up against the station building and sat on one of the platform benches with him in the sunshine, chatting until the next train came along. I was familiar with country railway stations and the comings and goings of soldiers.

Most of those small picturesque stations are gone now, along with the sweet railway lines that wound their way through the countryside linking them all together. Some of *the old routes have been made into cycle tracks, or places where people can walk, exercise or take their dogs.*

For almost thirty years, until recently, our family lived close to the disused railway track which once ran up to Stow-on-the-Wold and beyond. I walked along it with our dogs on most days. The cuttings and embankments are still plain to see, though trees now encroach on both sides and in many places knit together overhead to form cool green tunnels.

Often when I was walking, I thought about all the young men who were called up during the two world wars. The young men who travelled on this railway line and thousands of others just like it, before being sent away to fight. I thought about them leaving their much-loved homes and families, staring out of the train windows looking at this same flawless English countryside, these same woods and streams. All those young men who never came back, and who are remembered only by an inscription on one of the myriad white headstones in France, the Far East, Gallipoli and countless other cemeteries worldwide.

I love the lonely, disused railway tracks, but sometimes they are disturbing. Full of ghosts.

Down the Line

Down long-forgotten railway lines and over broken
  bridges,
Came the young men,
From vanished stations with frilled eaves,
Past coal yards and sidings,
Over points switched by signalmen unseen,
They came from valleys green,
From blackened cities, mean,
To battlefields, obscene.

We ruined tracks that run below,
We saw them go, we saw them go,
Don't let them hear the song of the track,
The clickety clack, the clackety clack,
They won't come back.

Drawn like single threads to forge a cable,
From factories and shops, from farm and stable,
Football teams, and banks and streets entire,
Through cuttings deep and scarred by summer fire,
Through tunnels dark, embankments steep, to face
the threat,
To learn the ways of rifle and of bayonet.

Hands which held the reins and steered the plough,
Must carry out more bloody service now,
Make hard the heart and subjugate the will,
To fire the bullet, stab and choke and kill,
For men, our country must more deeply delve,
Now some are fifty-six and some are twelve.*

You mothers on windswept platforms, crippled by
   the gash of fear,
Go home.
You aching sweetheart, bent and crying for your
   young man,
Go home.
You have shared a last embrace.
Hold it tenderly, remember it, safeguard and
   cherish it,
For it must last a lifetime.
And pity the straight-backed fathers, who weep alone.

Over continents this was enacted,
Young men from their loving homes extracted,
Faces white and yellow, brown and black,
Believing that, one day, they would go back.
In haunted carriages I see them yet,
Khaki-clad, with kitbag, cigarette,
Through dim-lit panes they see me, far below,
I look into their eyes and watch them go.

They weren't to know, as they travelled the lea,
The hideous scenes they were going to see,
The flames, the gas cloud drifting, pale,
In Ypres, the Somme and Passchendaele.
To draw a last despairing breath,
Man and beast in a dismal death.

Carved names that crumble soft away,
In churches and on crosses grey,
At cenotaphs where poppies fall,
Embrace the life denied them all.
In hamlet sweet and city loud,
I still the clamour of the crowd,
And mourn them from this heart of mine:
The soldiers, sailors, airmen fine,
The boys who travelled down the line.

* In April 1918 the Earl of Derby, Director-General of Recruiting, ordered that the age of recruits could be raised to fifty-six 'if the need arose'. Sidney Lewis was sent home August 1916, one year after joining up. He had run away to enlist when twelve years old and lied about his age. He was sent to the Somme and fought on the front for six weeks. His mother then discovered where he had gone, sent his birth certificate to the War Office and demanded his return.

I *was asked to write a poem to thank our emergency*
services – a piece which would recognise that the
work they do comes with colossal levels of stress, and
which emphasised how low manning levels and late-night
shifts mean great disruption to family life.

I was pleased to tackle this subject because, on the few
occasions I've had to call on them, the emergency services
have been vastly impressive and inspiring. Like most of us,
I feel safer knowing that they are all there at the end of the
phone when things go wrong.

Who Goes There?

Who goes there? To the accident, the robbery,
  the fire?
Who goes *towards* the danger in the city and
  the shire?
Who does the most unselfish work that any
  person can?
Not for fame or fortune, but to help their
  fellow man.

When shifts they are relentless, and the lack of
  sleep too rough,
And though we see our families, it's not for
  long enough,
When days are too exhausting for just pasting
  on the grin,
There are not many of us. Everybody's spread
  too thin.

The birthday party missed, the disappointment
  hard to mend,
The sports day and the carol concert Dad could
  not attend,
Mum, who couldn't make the parents' evening at
  the school.
Missed family occasions. And the hot date left
  to cool.

For the workload is increasing, and you're meant to
  never tire,
Of the boring and the bolshie and the damaged
  and the dire,
Of calming situations, and avoiding uppercuts,
To separate the man and wife who hate each
  other's guts.

Who walks towards the RTA when lights are
  flashing blue?
Whose torch lights up the wreck? It isn't me, thank
  God. Nor you.
Who washes down the carriageway, who knows
  what happened there?
Who knocks the door of the happy home, and
  leaves it in despair?

And who, in heavy, suffocating, heat-resistant kit,
Goes towards the fire, when all our instincts flee
  from it?
In factory or forest, or to pump away the flood,
And yet is big enough to save a cow stuck in
  the mud.

Who understands the blaze, and can predict its
  likely path?
And when the flames are gone, who must inspect
  the aftermath?
Investigate the places where the fire has held
  domain,
And sift the evidence. And rake the ashes for
  remains.

In the lottery of life, some folk live comfortable
  and nice,
Some have to live with exploitation, violence
  and vice,
Some fall through the net to live with
  hopelessness, despair,
But the people who protect us, they protect us
  everywhere.

They go into the mountains with their search dogs
    and their ropes,
Lifeboat crews in hostile seas man little orange
    boats,
And crawling underground into the flooded
    nightmare stark,
The cavers, in the claustrophobic, terrifying dark.

To the dirty underbelly with the spit and the
    abuse,
To the squat and to the alley, they all come to be
    of use,
To the sleeper on the street, the addict dying of
    despair,
To treat the alcoholic. Take the children into care.

How easy is it then, to wash away the memory,
Of the fury and the anguish that you didn't want
    to see?
Who consoles the comforter? What reassuring
    words,
Can sweep away the image: what was seen and
    what was heard.

A privilege for sure, that in this land of yours
    and mine,
By picking up the telephone and dialling 999,
Skilful people come to help the desperate, the
    lost,
Though to their own well-being, they are coming
    at a cost.

Thanks to all the people that we hope we never
    meet,
In vehicles we hope will never speed into our
    street,
The fire, police and ambulance, the lights, the
    sirens blare,
We never want to see you.
                But we thank God you are there.

Acknowledgements

Very special thanks to my literary agent Vivien Green of Sheil Land for her encouragement, excellent advice and always-supportive presence. I am immensely grateful to her.

Also to Ebury Press for their enthusiasm and help, to Anna Mrowiec, Charlotte Cole and all the team.

To Susan Hellard who agreed to illustrate these, my new poems, as she has so many in the past. I love her illustrations, both poignant and hilarious, and greatly admire her skill and perception.

To the brilliant Claire Jones, BBC radio producer and archetypal 'iron fist in the velvet glove', for persuading me to make another series of BBC Radio 4's *Ayres on the Air* when I didn't think I had enough ideas. The gentle encouraging (yet persistent!) voice on the end of the telephone meant that in the end I wrote far more material than I believed I could.

To the people who buy my books and to everyone who sells them, particularly the gallant independent bookstores in their towns and villages.

Lastly, to my husband Dudley Russell for his wise council and protection over many years. Thanks to him and to all my fantastic family, our sons, daughters-in-law and grandchildren.

Thank you for the laughs.

Index of First Lines

I

I am the dog who bit the ball, 16
I bought a jolly fishcake, 38
I don't know if there is a Heaven, 108
I had a little worm farm, it caused a lot of rows, 79
I like the sound of a crackly packet, 91
I'm all stocked up with Duty Free, 77
I'm such a happy person and my smile is like the sun, 96
I purchased a kiwi marked 'Perfectly Ripe', 28
I think I'll live upon the moon, 100
It seemed like such a good idea, a flash of inspiration, 10
I've got to find a document, whereabouts unknown, 1
I was skinny when I boarded but am now quite roly-poly,
    36
I went down to Salisbury, 105
I wish I had a bodyguard to keep me safe from harm, 102
I wish my man would start to doubt, 87
I wish you, little baby Archie, 106

L

Landed now and doors to manual, 74

M

Men once adored me, but now they are curt, 39
My granny was coshed at the cashpoint! 55

N

Now, my man is very clever, 21

O

P

R

S

T

W

What pillock hung the poo bag from the briar? 89
When I fancy fish and chips and wander down the pub, 6
Who goes there? To the accident, the robbery, the fire? 117